CLASSIC
JAPANESE RAMEN
AT HOME

100 Traditional Japanese
Recipes with simple ingredients

HANLEY PAGE

Disclaimer

The information contained in this eBook is meant to serve as a comprehensive collection of strategies that the author of this eBook has done research about. Summaries, strategies, tips and tricks are only recommendation by the author, and reading this eBook will not guarantee that one's results will exactly mirror the author's results. The author of the eBook has made all reasonable effort to provide current and accurate information for the readers of the eBook. The author and it's associates will not be held liable for any unintentional error or omissions that may be found. The material in the eBook may include information by third parties. Third party materials comprise of opinions expressed by their owners. As such, the author of the eBook does not assume responsibility or liability for any third party material or opinions. Whether because of the progression of the internet, or the unforeseen changes in company policy and editorial submission guidelines, what is stated as fact at the time of this writing may become outdated or inapplicable later.

TABLE OF CONTENTS

INTRODUCTION

The Japanese have always enjoyed the attention of the world, all thanks to their enviable technology array. And their cuisine is another area of great admiration by many but not everyone has a grasp of pantry creativity. Well, that is about to change because you will be toured around 100 incredible and easy Japanese ramen dishes to make at home. With this, you can finally close your eyes and enjoy endless Japanese aroma in the air.

Japanese cooking mainly includes the territorial and conventional nourishments of Japan, which have been developed through hundreds of years of political, monetary, and social changes. The customary cooking of Japan depends on rice with miso soup and different dishes; there is an accentuation on seasonal ingredients.

BREAKFAST

1. Ramen omelet

Servings: 6

Ingredients

- 2 (3 oz.) packages ramen noodles, cooked
- 6 eggs
- 1 red bell pepper, chopped
- 1 large carrot, grated
- 1/2 C. parmesan cheese, grated

Directions

a) Get a mixing bowl: Mix in it the eggs with 1 ramen seasoning packet.

b) Add the noodles, bell pepper and carrot. Mix them well.

c) Before you do anything else, preheat the oven to 356 F.

d) Grease a muffin tin with some butter or a cooking spray. Spoon the batter into the tins.

e) Top the muffins with the parmesan cheese. Cook the muffins in the oven for 16 minutes. Serve them warm. Enjoy.

2. Marinated eggs for ramen

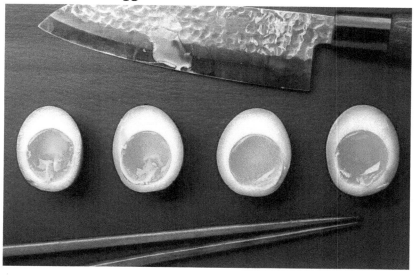

Servings: 1

Ingredients

- 6 eggs
- 1 tablespoon rice vinegar
- 2 tablespoons soy sauce
- 1 teaspoon sugar
- 1/2 teaspoons sesame oil

Directions

a) Place a pot over medium heat. Place in it the eggs and cover them with water. Cook them until they start boiling.

b) Turn off the heat and put on the lid. Let the eggs sit for 10 minutes. Once the time is up drain the eggs and place them in a bowl. Cover them with some cold water and let them sit for 6 minutes. Peel them and place them aside.

c) Get a small heavy saucepan: Whisk in it the vinegar, soy sauce, sugar, and sesame oil to make the marinade.

d) Cook them over medium heat until they start boiling. Turn off the heat and place the marinade aside until it becomes warm.

e) Place the eggs in a large mason jar and pour the marinade all over them. Seal it and place it aside to sit for 1 day.

f) Once the time is up, drain the eggs and serve them with your ramen.

g) Enjoy.

3. Bento ramen eggs

Servings: 4

Ingredients

- 6 large eggs
- 1tablespoons baking soda
- Seasoning sauce
- $\frac{1}{4}$ cup. Sake
- $\frac{1}{4}$ cup Mizkan Bonito flavored soup base or any soup base
- 5tablespoons soy sauce
- 4tablespoons mirin

Instructions

a) In a small saucepan, pour in water add the baking soda, bring to boil. Add the eggs and cook for 10 minutes when the water boils

b) In another saucepan, stir in all the sauce **Ingredients** and cook for 5 minutes. Turn out the heat and sit it for cooling

c) When the egg is done, remove and ice-cool it. Crack and peel the shell, place in a container

d) Pour the cooled sauce over the eggs, making sure the eggs are completed immersed in the sauce. Leave it in the refrigerator overnight

e) When ready, remove from refrigerator slice each into half, and serve

4. Hiroshima Okonomiyaki

Servings: 2

Ingredients:

- Water, two tablespoons
- Eggs, three
- Bacon, six strips
- Cabbage, 150g
- Okonomiyaki flour, half cup
- Okonomiyaki sauce, two tablespoons
- Bonito flakes, as required
- Yakisoba noodles, two cups
- Pickled ginger, one teaspoon
- Aonori seaweed, as required

Method:

a) Mix the okonomiyaki flour with the water, and one egg until you have a smooth batter with no lumps.

b) Add just under half the batter to a pan in a nice even circle.

c) Add half of the cabbage and half of the bean sprouts on top of the batter and then bacon.

d) Pour one tablespoon of the batter on the top of the mix and let cook for about ten minutes before flipping.

e) cook one serving of yakisoba & move the okonomiyaki on top of the noodles.

f) Crack an egg in a bowl and break the yolk before pouring in the first pan to the side of the okonomiyaki.

g) Place the okonomiyaki over the egg and leave to cook for two minutes.

h) Garnish and serve.

APPETIZERS & SNACKS

5. Minty noodles cookies

Servings: 24

Ingredients

- 4 (3 oz.) packets ramen noodles, uncooked

- 1 (16 oz.) bags dark chocolate chips

- 12-14 drops peppermint extract

- 1-2 drop spear mint extract

- 1-2 drop wintergreen extract

- 24 lollipop sticks

- 1/2 teaspoons butter (optional)

Directions

a) Break the noodles into pieces and place it in a mixing bowl. Place a pot over low heat. Stir in it the chocolate chips with butter until they melt.

b) Stir in the mint extract. Cook them for 1 minutes. Pour the mix all over the noodles and mix them well.

c) Use a large tablespoons to spoon the mix in the shape of cookies on a lined up baking sheet. place the pan in the fridge for at least 1 h. Serve your cookies with your favorite toppings.

d) Enjoy.

6. Fried ramen rings

Servings: 1

Ingredients

- Batter for Frying, reserve 2 C.

- 1 C. self-rising flour

- 1 teaspoon salt

- 1/4 teaspoons pepper

- 2 eggs, beaten

- 1 C. beer, or milk

- Onions

- 2 (3 oz.) packages ramen noodles, packet reserved oil, for frying

- 1 large Vidalia onion, ringed

Directions

a) Get a large mixing bowl: Whisk in it the flour, eggs, beer, a pinch of salt and pepper.

b) Get a food processor: Cut the one ramen in half and process it in it until it becomes ground. Add it to the flour batter and mix them well. Finely crush the other ramen and place it in a shallow dish. Add to it the seasoning packet and mix them well.

c) Place a large pan over medium heat. Fill 3/4 inch of it with oil and heat it.

d) Coat the onion rings with the flour batter and dip them in the crushed noodles mix. Place them in the hot oil and cook them until they become golden brown.

e) Serve your onion rings with your favorite dip.

f) Enjoy.

7. Faux pepperoni ramen pizza

Servings: 6

Ingredients

- 1 (3 oz.) packages ramen noodles, any flavor

- 1 tablespoon olive oil

- 1 (14 oz.) jars spaghetti sauce

- 1 C. low-fat mozzarella cheese, shredded

- 3 oz. turkey pepperoni

- 1/2 teaspoons dried oregano

Directions

a) Before you do anything, preheat the oven broiler.

b) Prepare the noodles according to the instructions on the package without the seasoning packet. Drain it.

c) Place a large oven proof pan over medium heat. Heat the oil in it. Sauté in it the noodles and press it to the bottom of it for 2 minutes to make the crust.

d) Pour the sauce all over the noodles and top it with 2 oz. pepperoni slices. Sprinkle the cheese on top followed by the remaining pepperoni and oregano.

e) Transfer the pan to the oven and cook them for 2 to 3 minutes or until the cheese melts.

f) Allow your pizza to lose the heat for 6 minutes. serve it.

g) Enjoy.

8. Thai ramen beef satay

Servings: 4

Ingredients

Marinade

- 2 tablespoons soy sauce

- 2 tablespoons lime juice

- 1 1/2 teaspoons sugar

- 1 1/2 teaspoons fresh ginger, grated, peeled

- 1 garlic clove, grated (optional)

- 1/4 teaspoons red pepper flakes (optional)

- 2 lbs flank steaks, thinly sliced against the grain

Peanut Ramen Glaze

- 1 tablespoon lime juice

- 1 teaspoon sugar

- 1 teaspoon fresh ginger, grated and peeled

- 1/3 C. creamy peanut butter

- 1/3 C. water

- 1 tablespoon soy sauce

- 1/4 teaspoons red pepper flakes (optional)

- 1/4 C. roasted peanuts, chopped

- 3 green onions, sliced

- vegetable oil, for grill

- 2 (3 oz.) packages ramen noodles, cooked, packet removed

Directions

a) Place 12 wooden skewers in some water and let them sit for 16 minutes. Get a roasting pan: Mix in it 2 tablespoons each soy sauce and lime juice and 1 1/2 teaspoons each sugar and ginger, garlic

and/or 1/4 teaspoons optional red
pepper flakes to make the marinade.

b) Add the beef slices to the marinade and
toss them to coat. Place them aside to
sit for 12 minutes.

c) Get a food processor: Combine in it 1
tablespoon lime juice, 1 teaspoon sugar,
and 1 teaspoon ginger with peanut butter
and 1/3 C. water. Process them until they
become smooth.

d) Add the rest of the soy sauce and
process them again. Pour the mix in small
mixing bowl.

e) Stir in it the chopped peanuts and green
onions and optional remaining 1/4
teaspoons of red pepper flakes to make
the sauce. Before you do anything else
preheat the grill and grease it.

f) Drain the beef slices and thread them
into the wooden skewers. Cook the beef
slices on the grill for 4 to 5 minutes on
each side.

g) Spoon the noodles into serving bowls. Drizzle the peanut sauce over it and top it with the grilled beef. Serve them hot. Enjoy.

9. Mock ramen pot pie

Servings: 4

Ingredients

- 2 (3 oz.) packages ramen noodles
- 1 lb ground beef
- 1 (15 oz.) cans sweet corn
- 1/2 C. onion, chopped
- vegetable oil

Directions

a) Before you do anything preheat the oven to 350 F.

b) Prepare the noodles according to the **Directions** on the package. Place a large pan over medium heat. Heat a splash of oil in it. Cook in it the beef with onion for 12 minutes.

c) Spread the mix in the bottom of a greased baking pan. Top it with the sweet corn and the ramen noodles after draining it.

d) Place the casserole in the oven and cook it for 14 to 16 minutes. Serve it

MAIN COURSE

10. Ramen Noodle Skillet with Steak

Servings: 2

Ingredients:

- Onion, one
- Carrots, half cup
- Ground beef, half pound
- Canola oil, one tablespoon
- Ketchup, two tablespoons
- Salt and pepper, to taste
- Corn starch, one teaspoon
- Beef broth, one cup
- Sake, one tablespoon
- Boiled egg, one
- Worcestershire sauce, one tablespoon

Directions:

a) In a large skillet over medium-high heat, heat oil.

b) Add steak and sear until your desired completion, about five minutes per side for medium, then transfer to a cutting board and let it rest for five minutes, and then slice it.

c) In a small bowl, whisk together soy sauce, garlic, lime juice, honey, and cayenne until combined and set aside.

d) Add onion, peppers, and broccoli to skillet and cook until tender, then add soy sauce mixture and stir until fully coated.

e) Add cooked ramen noodles and steak and toss until combined.

11. Cheesy Ramen Carbonara

Servings: 4

Ingredients:

- Dashi, one cup
- Olive oil, one tablespoon
- Bacon slices, six
- Salt, as required
- Minced garlic, two
- Parsley, as required
- Parmesan cheese, half cup
- Milk, two tablespoons
- Eggs, two
- Ramen pack, three

Method:

a) Combine all the **Ingredients**.

b) Boil noodles according to package instructions.

c) Save a quarter cup of cooking water to loosen sauce later, if needed. Drain noodles and toss with olive oil so that they do not stick.

d) Heat medium skillet over medium heat. Cook bacon pieces until brown and crisp. Add the noodles to the skillet and toss with the bacon until the noodles are coated in the bacon fat.

e) Beat eggs with fork and mix in parmesan cheese. Pour egg-cheese mixture to skillet and toss with bacon and noodles.

12. Four-Ingredient ramen

Servings: 2

Ingredients

- 1 (3 oz.) packages ramen noodles, any flavor

- 2 C. water

- 2 tablespoons butter

- 1/4 C. milk

Directions

a) Place a pot over medium heat and fill most of it with water. Cook it until it starts boiling.

b) Stir in it the noodles and let it cook for 4 minutes. discard the water and place the noodles in an empty pot.

c) Stir in it the milk with butter and seasoning mix. Cook them for 3 to 5 minutes over low heat until they become creamy. Serve it warm. Enjoy.

13. Ramen lasagna

Servings: 4

Ingredients

- 2 (3 oz.) packages ramen noodles

- 1 lb ground beef

- 3 eggs

- 2 C. shredded cheese

- 1 tablespoon minced onion

- 1 C. spaghetti sauce

Directions

a) Before you do anything preheat the oven to 325 F.

b) Place a large skillet over medium heat. Cook in it the beef with 1 seasoning packet and onion for 10 minutes.

c) Transfer the beef to a greased baking pan. Whisk the eggs and cook them in the same pan until they are done.

d) Top the beef with 1/2 C. of shredded cheese followed by the cooked eggs and another 1/2 C. of cheese.

e) Cook the ramen noodles according to the instructions on the package. Drain it and toss it with the spaghetti sauce.

f) Spread the mix all over the cheese layer. Top it with the remaining cheese. Cook it in the oven for 12 minutes. serve your lasagna warm. Enjoy.

14. Lemongrass ramen with duck

Servings: 4

Ingredients

- 5 C. water
- 4 C. chicken stock
- 2 red chilies, seeded and halved
- 8 slices ginger
- 3 tablespoons lemon juice
- 3 stalks lemongrass
- 2 sprigs coriander
- 1 Chinese barbecued duck, deboned and chopped
- 4 shallots, chopped
- 150 g dried ramen noodles
- bean sprouts, to garnish
- red chile, to garnish
- coriander, to garnish
- 3 bunches bok choy

- salt

- white pepper

Directions

a) Place a large saucepan over medium heat. Stir in it the water with stock and bring them to a simmer.

b) Crush the lemongrass with coriander and add them to the pot with the galangal, chilis and lime juice. Let them cook for 22 minutes. Once the time is up, pour the mix in a colander and drain it. Stir the drained mix aside.

c) Add the drain liquid to the saucepan. Stir in the shallot with the duck and cook for 5 minutes.

d) Prepare the noodles according to the **Directions** on the package without the seasoning packet. Stir the bok choy into the soup and let it cook for an extra 6 minutes.

e) Serve your soup hot with your favorite toppings.

f) Enjoy.

15. Fermented sichuan noodles

Servings: 2

Ingredients

Sauce

- 1/2 tablespoons fermented black beans

- 2 tablespoons chili bean paste

- 1/2 tablespoons Shaoxing wine or 1/2 tablespoons dry sherry

- 1 teaspoon soy sauce

- 1 teaspoon sesame oil

- 1 teaspoon sugar

- 1/2 teaspoons ground Sichuan pepper

Noodles

- 1 tablespoon peanut oil or 1 tablespoon vegetable oil

- 4 oz. ground pork or 4 oz. ground beef

- 2 scallions, white green parts separated chopped

- 1 garlic clove, minced
- 1 teaspoon fresh ginger, minced
- 3 C. chicken stock
- 1 lb tofu, cubes
- 2 (4 oz.) packages ramen noodles, packet removed

Directions

a) Get a small mixing bowl: Crush in it the black beans with chili bean paste, rice wine, soy sauce, sesame oil, sugar, and Sichuan pepper until they become smooth.

b) Place a large pan over medium heat. Heat the oil in it. Brown in it the pork for 3 minutes.

c) Stir in the scallion whites, garlic, and ginger and cook them for 1 minute over low heat.

d) Stir in the black bean mix with the broth into the pan. Cook them until they start boiling. Lower the heat and stir in the tofu. Let them cook for 6 minutes.

e) Prepare the noodles according to the **Directions** on the package.

f) Spoon it into serving bowls and top it with tofu mix.

g) Serve your noodles bowels hot.

h) Enjoy.

16. Japanese teriyaki zoodles stir fry

Servings: 4

Ingredients

- 2 tablespoons vegetable oil
- 1 medium onion, thinly sliced
- 2 medium zucchinis, cut into thin strips
- 2 tablespoons teriyaki sauce
- 1 tablespoon soy sauce
- 1 tablespoon toasted sesame seeds
- ground black pepper

Directions

a) Place a large pan over medium heat. Heat the oil in it. Add the onion and cook it for 6 minutes.

b) Stir in the zucchini and cook them for 2 minutes. Add the remaining **Ingredients** and cook them for 6 minutes. Serve your stir fry right away. Enjoy.

17. Lunch box noodles

Servings: 1

Ingredients

- 1 (3 oz.) packages ramen noodles
- 1/2 C. frozen peas
- 1 tablespoon butter
- 1 tablespoon parmesan cheese

Directions

a) Bring a large saucepan of water to a boil. Crush the noodles and stir it into the hot water with the peas.

b) Cook them until they start boiling. Pour the mix in a colander and discard the water.

c) Get a mixing bowl: Toss in it the hot noodles mix with the butter, parmesan, and 1/3 of the ramen's seasoning packet. Serve your noodles bowls warm.

d) Enjoy.

18. Hawaiian ramen skillet

Servings: 2

Ingredients

- 6 oz. Spam
- 1 green bell pepper, stir fried, chopped
- 1/2 C. onion, diced
- 1 (3 oz.) packages ramen noodles
- 1 clove garlic, peeled and diced
- 1/4 teaspoons salt
- 1/4 teaspoons ground black pepper
- 1 tablespoon olive oil
- 1/2 teaspoons butter

Directions

a) Place a large saucepan over medium heat. Cook in it 2 C. of water until they start boiling.

b) Place in it the noodles without the seasoning packet. Drain it and place it aside.

c) Place a large skillet over medium heat. Heat in it the butter until it melts with olive oil. Cook in them the onion for 3 minutes.

d) Stir in the Spam, bell pepper, and the garlic. Cook them for 4 minutes.

e) Stir in 1/2 C. of the noodles cooking liquid with the drained noodles.

f) Let it sit for 1 minute then serve it warm.

g) Enjoy.

19. Sweet ramen with tofu

Servings: 1

Ingredients

- 1 package chicken-flavored ramen noodles

- 2 C. water

- 2 tablespoons vegetable oil

- 3 slices tofu, 1/4 inch thick

- 2 C. soy bean sprouts

- 1/2 small zucchini, thinly sliced

- 2 green onions, sliced

- 1/2 C. sweet green pea pods

- flour

- seasoning salt

- sesame oil

Directions

a) Slice each tofu piece into 3 chunks. Dust them with some flour. Place a large skillet over medium heat. Heat 1 tablespoon of oil in it.

b) Cook in it the tofu for 1 to 2 minutes on each side. Drain it and place it aside. Heat a splash of oil in the same pan. Sauté in it the veggies for 6 minutes. Place them aside.

c) Cook the noodles. Stir in it the seasoning packet.

d) Place a large skillet over medium heat. Heat a splash of oil in it.

e) Cook in it the bean sprouts for 1 minutes.

f) Lay the fried bean sprouts in the bottom of serving bowl. Top it with the ramen, cooked veggies and tofu. Serve them hot. Enjoy.

20. Ginger beef ramen

Servings: 4

Ingredients

- 14 oz. dried ramen noodles
- 12 oz. beef sirloin, half frozen to make slicing easier
- 1 1/2 quarts chicken stock
- 1 inch piece gingerroot, roughly sliced
- 2 garlic cloves, halved
- 2 tablespoons sake
- 3 tablespoons shoyu, plus
- 1 tablespoon shoyu, for stir-frying
- 1 bok choy, trimmed and thinly shredded
- 2 tablespoons peanut oil
- 8 dried shiitake mushrooms, soaked
- sea salt, to taste
- fresh ground black pepper, to taste

Directions

a) Prepare the noodles according to the instructions on the package.

b) Discard the water and place the noodles aside.

c) Slice the beef into thin slices.

d) Place a large saucepan over medium heat. Heat the stock in it. Stir in it the ginger with garlic and cook them for 12 minutes over low heat.

e) Once the time is up, drain the ginger with garlic and discard them. Add the sake, shoyu and salt and pepper to the broth.

f) Place a large pan over medium heat. Heat 1 tablespoon of oil in it. Sauté in it the baby bok choy for 3 minutes. Drain it and place it aside.

g) Heat the remaining oil in the same skillet. Sauté in it the beef with mushroom for 4 minutes. Stir into them the shoyu with a pinch of salt and pepper.

h) Stir the noodles in some hot water to heat it then drain it. Place it in serving bowls then top it with the beef, shiitake, and bok choy. Pour the chicken broth all over them. Serve it right away.

i) Enjoy.

21. Ramen roulade

Servings: 6

Ingredients

- 1 1/2 lbs flank steaks
- 3 tablespoons seasoning salt
- pepper
- 1 egg, beaten
- 1 tablespoon water
- 1 tablespoon flour
- 1 (3 oz.) packages Top Ramen noodles, packet discarded toothpick
- 2 tablespoons steak sauce

Directions

a) Before you do anything, preheat the oven to 350 F.

b) Place 2 flank steaks on a broad. Flatten them with a kitchen hammer. Season the steak pieces with the McCormick All

Seasoning, a pinch of salt and pepper on both sides.

c) Get a small mixing bowl: MIX in it the eggs with water. Add the flour and mix them well.

d) Lather the mix all over 1 side of the steak pieces. Break the ramen into pieces and lay it all over the steak pieces.

e) Roll the steaks over the filling and seal them with toothpicks. Place the steaks roulades on a greased baking sheet. Cook them in the oven for 42 to 46 minutes.

f) Drizzle the steak sauce over the roulades and cook them for an extra 12 minutes. allow them to rest for 12 minutes then serve them with your favorite toppings.

22. Louisiana Shrimp ramen

Servings: 1

Ingredients

- 1 (3 oz.) packages shrimp flavor ramen noodle soup

- 6 large shrimp, skin and veins removed

- 1 tablespoon butter

- 1/4 teaspoons garlic powder

- 1 teaspoon creole seasoning

- 1/4 teaspoons black pepper

- 1/2 teaspoons hot sauce

Directions

a) Cut the noodles in half and prepare it according to the **Directions** on the package without the seasoning packet.

b) Place a large skillet over medium heat. Melt the butter in it. Sauté in it the shrimp with garlic powder, creole seasoning, and black pepper for 6 minutes.

c) Pour the noodles with 1/4 C. of the cooking liquid in a serving bowl.

d) Top it with the shrimp and hot sauce then serve it warm.

e) Enjoy.

23. Sunflower ramen with vinaigrette

Servings: 8

Ingredients

Ramen

- 16 oz. shredded cabbage, or coleslaw mix

- 2/3 C. sunflower seeds

- 1/2 C. slivered almonds

- 3 bags oriental-flavor instant ramen noodles, crunched, uncooked, packet saved

- 1 bunch green onion, chopped

Vinaigrette

- 1/2 C. oil

- 3 tablespoons red wine vinegar

- 3 tablespoons sugar

- 2 teaspoons pepper

- 3 packages seasoning from oriental-flavor instant ramen noodles

Directions

a) Get a large mixing bowl: Toss in it the salad **Ingredients**.

b) Get a small mixing bowl: Whisk in it the dressing **Ingredients**.

c) Drizzle the dressing over the salad and toss them to coat. Serve it right away.

d) Enjoy.

24. Shoyu Ramen

Serving: 4

Ingredients:

- Chashu, one cup
- Nitamago, as required
- Shiitake, as required
- La-yu, as required
- Nori, half cup
- Ramen, four packs
- Dashi, half cup

Directions:

a) In a pot of salted boiling water, cook ramen, stirring with tongs or chopsticks until cooked, about one minute.

b) In a small saucepan over medium heat, warm dashi and shiitake until barely simmering.

c) Cook for one minute and remove from heat.

d) Set shiitake aside.

e) Add dashi and noodles to serving bowl.

f) Top with chashu, nitamago, shiitake, green onion, a drizzle of la-yu, and nori, if desired.

25. Miso Ramen

Serving: 2

Ingredients:

- Miso paste, 1 tablespoon
- Mix vegetables, 1 cup
- Ramen, 2 packs
- Soy sauce, 1 tablespoon

Directions:

a) Cook the ramen, and boil the vegetables.
b) Now mix all the remaining **Ingredients**, and serve hot.

26. Simple Homemade Chicken Ramen

Serving: 2

Ingredients:

- Chicken, one cup
- Ramen noodles, two packs
- Oil, one teaspoon
- Salt and pepper to taste

Directions:

a) Cook the ramen, and chicken.
b) Now mix all the other **Ingredients**, and serve hot.

27. Vegetarian Ramen

Serving: 2

Ingredients:

- Mix vegetables, one cup
- Ramen noodles, two packs
- Oil, one teaspoon
- Salt and pepper to taste

Directions:

a) Cook the ramen, and vegetables.
b) Now mix all the other **Ingredients**, and serve hot.

28. Ramen Noodles

Serving: 2

Ingredients:

- Ramen noodles, two packs
- Miso paste, two tablespoons
- Soy Sauce, one tablespoon

Directions:

a) Mix all the **Ingredients** together, and cook well for ten minutes.
b) Your dish is ready to be served.

29. Pork Ramen

Serving: 2

Ingredients:

- Pork meat, one cup
- Ramen noodles, two packs
- Oil, one teaspoon
- Salt and pepper to taste

Directions:

a) Cook the ramen, and pork meat.
b) Now mix all the **Ingredients**, and serve hot.

30. Instant Ramen

Serving: 2

Ingredients:

- Instant ramen noodles, two packs
- Instant spice mix, two tablespoons
- Water, three cups

Directions:

a) Mix all the **Ingredients** together and cook for ten minutes.

b) Your dish is ready to be served.

31. American ground beef ramen

Servings: 4

Ingredients

- 1 lb ground beef, drained
- 3 (3 oz.) packets beef-flavor ramen noodles
- 5 C. boiling water
- 1/4-1/2 C. water
- 1 (16 oz.) cans corn
- 1 (16 oz.) cans peas
- 1/4 C. soy sauce
- 1/2 teaspoons ground red pepper
- 1 dash cinnamon
- 2 teaspoons sugar

Directions

a) Place a large pan over medium heat. Heat a splash of oil in it. Add the beef and cook it for 8 minutes. Place it aside.

b) Place a large saucepan over medium heat. Heat 5 C. of water in it until it starts boiling. Cook in it the noodles for 3 to 4 minutes.

c) Remove the noodles from the water and stir it into the skillet with the beef.

d) Add the water, corn, peas, soy sauce, red pepper, cinnamon, sugar and 1 and a half of the seasoning packets. Toss them to coat.

e) Let them cook for 6 minutes while stirring often. Serve your ramen Skillet Hot.

32. Kimchee noodles

Servings: 2

Ingredients

- 1 1/2 C. kimchee
- 1 (3 oz.) packages oriental-flavor instant ramen noodles
- 1 (12 oz.) packages Spam, cubed
- 2 tablespoons vegetable oil

Directions

a) Cook the noodles according to the instructions on the package. Place the pan over medium heat. Heat the oil in it. Sauté in it the spam pieces for 3 minutes.

b) Stir in the noodles after draining it and cook them for an extra 3 minutes.

c) Stir in the kimchee and cook them for 2 minutes. serve your noodles warm.

33. Roasted miso noodles

Servings: 2

Ingredients

- 4 large eggs, hard boiled
- 1 tablespoon unsalted butter
- 1 C. sweet corn
- 1 tablespoon olive oil
- 8 oz. fresh spinach
- 1 quart chicken stock
- 1 teaspoon red miso
- 6 oz. ramen noodles
- 6 oz. cooked chicken
- 4 green onions, thinly sliced
- 1 teaspoon toasted sesame oil, for drizzling

Directions

a) Place a small saucepan over medium heat. Melt in it the butter. Add the corn with a pinch of salt and pepper then heat them though. Place it aside.

b) Place a large pan over medium heat. Heat the oil in it. Add to it the spinach and cook them for 2 minutes. Place it aside.

c) Place a large saucepan over medium heat. Heat in it the chicken stock until it starts boiling. Add to it the miso paste and mix them well.

d) Stir in the noodles and cook it for 3 minutes. Spoon the noodles into serving bowls.

e) Top it with the corn, spinach and chicken. Garnish it with the green onions, sesame oil and eggs. Serve them hot. Enjoy.

34. Tropical curry ramen

Servings: 4

Ingredients

- 2 (3 oz.) packages ramen noodles
- 1 tablespoon vegetable oil
- 1 teaspoon crushed red pepper flakes
- 2 garlic cloves, minced
- 1 C. shredded cabbage
- 1 C. thinly sliced mixed mushrooms
- 1 C. chopped broccoli
- 1 tablespoon peanut butter
- 1 tablespoon soy sauce
- 1 tablespoon brown sugar
- 1 C. coconut milk
- 1 teaspoon curry powder
- 1 teaspoon sambal oelek
- 1 lime, juice of

- 1/2 teaspoons salt

- 1 tablespoon crushed peanuts

- 1/4 C. chopped cilantro

- lime wedge

Directions

a) Prepare the noodles according to the **Directions** on the package without the seasoning packets. Drain the noodles and reserve the cooking liquid.

b) Place a large pan over medium heat. Heat the oil in it. Sauté in it the garlic with red pepper for 40 seconds.

c) Stir in the cabbage, mushrooms and broccoli. Add the veggies and cook them for 6 minutes. Stir the noodles into the pan and place them aside.

d) Place another pan over medium heat. Stir in it the peanut butter, soy sauce, brown sugar, coconut milk, curry powder, sambal oelek and salt. Cook them until they start boiling.

e) Add the cooked noodles and veggies and stir them to coat. Stir in 1/4 C. of the cooking liquid. Cook them until they mix becomes thick. Let the ramen skillet rest for 6 minutes.

f) Top the ramen skillet with the cilantro and peanuts then serve them hot. Enjoy.

35. Hot shot of ramen

Servings: 2

Ingredients

- 1 1/2 C. water
- 1 small yellow onion, finely diced
- 1 celery rib, finely diced
- 6 baby carrots, julienne
- 1 (3 oz.) packages ramen noodles, broken
- 1 (5 1/2 oz.) cans sardines in tomato sauce
- 2-3 dashes hot sauce

Directions

a) Place a large saucepan of water over medium heat. Stir in it the water, onion, celery, and carrots. Cook them for 12 minutes. Stir in the noodles and cook it for 3 to 4 minutes.

b) Stir the sardines with tomato, and hot sauce into the saucepan. Serve it hot with your favorite toppings.

36. Ramen dinner

Servings: 1

Ingredients

- 1 (6 oz.) cans tuna in vegetable oil

- 1 (3 oz.) packets ramen noodles, any flavor

- 1/2 C. frozen mixed vegetables

Directions

a) Place a large skillet over medium heat. Heat in it a splash of oil.

b) Cook in it the tuna for 2 to 3 minutes.

c) Prepare the ramen noodles according to the **Directions** on the package with the veggies.

d) Remove the noodles and veggies from the water and transfer them to the pan. Stir into them the seasoning packet and cook them for 2 to 3 minutes.

e) Serve your ramen tuna warm.

37. Sweet & spicy ramen stir fry

Servings: 4

Ingredients

- 1 (14 oz.) packages extra firm tofu, cubed

- 8 teaspoons soy sauce

- 2 tablespoons vegetable oil

- 8 oz. shiitake mushrooms, sliced thin

- 2 teaspoons Asian chili sauce

- 3 garlic cloves, minced

- 1 tablespoon grated fresh ginger

- 3 1/2 C. low sodium chicken broth

- 4 (3 oz.) packages ramen noodles, packets discarded

- 3 tablespoons cider vinegar

- 2 teaspoons sugar

- 1 (6 oz.) bags Baby Spinach

Directions

a) Use some paper towels to pat the tofu dry.

b) Get a mixing bowl: Stir in it the tofu with 2 teaspoons of soy sauce.

c) Place a large pan over medium heat. Heat 1 tablespoon of oil in it. Sauté in it the tofu for 2 to 3 minutes on each side then drain it and place it aside.

d) Heat the rest of the oil in the same skillet. Sauté in it the mushroom for 5 minutes. Add the chili sauce, garlic, and ginger. Let them cook for 40 seconds.

e) Crush the ramen into pieces. Stir it into the pan with the broth and cook them for 3 minutes or until the ramen is done.

f) Add 2 tablespoons soy sauce, vinegar, and sugar. Add the spinach and cook them for 2 to 3 minutes or until it welts.

g) Fold the tofu into the noodles then serve it warm.

38. Parmesan tuna ramen

Servings: 1

Ingredients

- 1 (3 oz.) packages chicken-flavored ramen noodles

- 1 1/2 C. water

- 1 (6 oz.) canned tuna

- 1-3 tablespoons parmesan cheese

- 1 tablespoon butter

- parsley flakes

- black pepper

Directions

a) Get a large serving bowl: Pour in it the water.

b) Crush the noodles and add it to the water with the seasoning packet.

c) Place it in the microwave and cook it for 5 minutes.

d) Stir in the Tuna, Parmesan, Butter, Pepper. Serve it hot.

e) Enjoy.

39. Ramen steak skillet

Servings: 4

Ingredients

- 1 lb beef round tip steak, stripped

- 2 cloves garlic, minced

- 1 tablespoon light sesame oil

- 1/4 teaspoons ground red pepper

- 1 (3 oz.) packages ramen noodles

- 1 (1 lb) package broccoli, carrots and water chestnuts

- 1 teaspoon light sesame oil

- 1 (4 1/2 oz.) jars mushrooms, drained

- 1 tablespoon soy sauce

Directions

a) Get a mixing bowl: Stir in it the beef strips, garlic, one tablespoon sesame oil and ground red pepper.

b) Place a pot over medium heat. Cook in it 2 C. of water until it starts boiling. Crush the noodles into 3 portions.

c) Stir it in the pot with the veggies and cook them until they start boiling. Lower the heat and cook them for an extra 3 minutes.

d) Pour the mix in a colander to remove the water. Place the noodles and veggies mix back into the pot.

e) Add the seasoning packet and stir them well.

f) Place a large pan over medium heat. Heat 1 teaspoon of sesame oil in it.

g) Cook in it the beef slices for 4 to 5 minutes or until they are done.

h) Stir the ramen and veggies mix into the skillet with the mushrooms and soy sauce. Cook them for an extra 3 minutes. Serve your skillet warm.

40. Teriyaki ramen bowls

Servings: 6

Ingredients

- 1 1/2 lbs salmon fillets, skinned and boned salt & black pepper

- 5 tablespoons teriyaki marinade

- vegetable oil, for rubbing

- 2 tablespoons red wine vinegar

- 1/4 C. sweet chili sauce

- 6 tablespoons Asian fish sauce

- 3 tablespoons fresh ginger, grated

- 1 lb soba noodles

- 1 tablespoon instant bouillon granules

- 1/2 C. scallion, thinly sliced

- 1 1/2 C. Spinach

- 1 tablespoon sesame seeds, toasted

Directions

a) Sprinkle some salt and pepper over the salmon fillets.

b) Get a large zip lock bag: Combine in it the salmon fillets with the teriyaki marinade. Seal the bag and shake it to coat. To make the chili sauce:

c) Get a small mixing bowl: Mix in it the vinegar, chili sauce, fish sauce and ginger. Place it aside.

d) Prepare the noodles according to the **Directions** on the package without the seasoning packet.

e) Remove the salmon fillets from the marinade and coat them with some oil.

f) Place a large pan over medium heat and heat it though. Cook in it the salmon fillet for 3 to 4 minutes on each side.

g) Add half of the salmon marinade to the pan and coat them with it.

h) Place them aside to sit for 6 minutes.

i) Cut the salmon into chunks then add to it the spinach with a pinch of salt and pepper. Cook them for 2 to 3 minutes.

j) Place a large saucepan over medium heat. Cook 6 C. of water in it until they start boiling. Add to it the bouillon powder and the white scallion pieces.

k) Reduce the heat and place the pot aside to make the broth.

l) Drain the noodles and place it in serving bowls. Pour over it the hot broth then top it with the salmon fillets. Enjoy.

41. Chili coconut ramen

Servings: 1

Ingredients

- 1 (3 oz.) packages ramen noodles
- 2 tablespoons peanut butter
- 1 teaspoon low sodium soy sauce
- 1 1/2 teaspoons chili-garlic sauce
- 2-3 tablespoons hot water
- 2 tablespoons sweetened flaked coconut

Garnish

- broccoli floret
- peanuts
- shredded carrot

Directions

a) Prepare the noodles according to the **Directions** on the package while discarding the seasoning packet.

b) Get a large mixing bowl: Beat in it the peanut butter, half of the seasoning packet, soy sauce, chili-garlic sauce, 2-3 tablespoons of hot water until they become smooth.

c) Add the noodles to the bowl and toss them to coat. Serve your noodles.

d) Enjoy.

42. Ramen green bean stir fry

Servings: 6

Ingredients

- 1 1/2 lbs fresh green beans

- 2 (3 oz.) packages ramen noodles

- 1/2 C. vegetable oil

- 1/3 C. toasted almond

- salt, as needed

- black pepper, as needed

Directions

a) Trim the green beans and slice them into 3 to 4 inches pieces. Place the green beans in a steamer and cook them until they become soft.

b) Get a large skillet. Stir in it the oil with 1 seasoning packet.

c) Crush 1 packet of noodles and stir it into the skillet. Add the steamed green beans and cook them for 3 to 4 minutes.

d) Adjust the seasoning of your stir fry then serve it warm.

e) Enjoy.

43. Shoyu ramen

Servings: 2

Ingredients

- 2 boneless skinless chicken breasts
- 2 tablespoons sesame oil
- 3 tablespoons shoyu
- 1 tablespoon rice vinegar
- 1 garlic clove, minced
- 2 teaspoons honey
- 2 (3 oz.) packages ramen noodles
- 1/3 C. shoyu
- 1/3 C. rice vinegar, unseasoned
- 2 teaspoons ground ginger
- 2 tablespoons honey
- 1 piece konbu
- 1 C. frozen broccoli

Directions

a) Slice the chicken breasts into bite size pieces.

b) Place a large pan over medium heat. Heat 3 tablespoons the sesame oil with 3 tablespoons shoyu, 1 tablespoon of the vinegar, 1 clove of garlic, and 2 teaspoons of honey. Stir them until they are heated though.

c) Stir the chicken into the pan. Cook it for 6 to 8 minutes or until it is done. Place a large saucepan over medium heat. Stir in it the remaining shoyu, vinegar, ginger, and honey. Stir enough water that can cover the noodles.

d) Heat them though until they honey melts. Add the veggies with konbu and bring them to a boil.

e) Once the time is up, discard the konbu and stir in the noodles. Cook them for 4 minutes. Spoon the ramen into serving bowls. Top it with the sweet chicken and serve it warm.

44. Broccoli and oyster ramen

Servings: 4

Ingredients

- 1 lb boneless beef top sirloin steak

- 1 tablespoon soy sauce

- 1 tablespoon apple juice

- 2 teaspoons cornstarch

- 2 (3 oz.) packages beef-flavor ramen noodles

- 4 C. boiling water

- 2 tablespoons olive oil

- 1 onion, chopped

- 3 C. frozen broccoli florets, thawed and drained

- 3 tablespoons oyster sauce

- 1 tablespoon cornstarch

Directions

a) Place the steak in the freezer until it is partially frozen then thinly slice it.

b) Get a large mixing bowl: Whisk in it the soy sauce, apple juice and 2 teaspoons cornstarch. Stir the beef into the mix.

c) Get a large mixing bowl: Crush the noodles into pieces stir it in it with the 1 seasoning packet.

d) Add 4 C. of water to the bowl and stir them. Cover the bowl and place it aside.

e) Place a large pan over high heat. Heat the oil in it. Sauté in it the beef for 3 minutes. Stir in the broccoli and cook it for 4 minutes.

f) Stir the beef into the skillet and cook them for 8 to 12 minutes. Get a small mixing bowl: Whisk in it 1 C. of the ramen soaking liquid, oyster sauce, and 1 tablespoon cornstarch.

g) Remove the noodles from the water and stir it into the skillet with oyster mix. Cook them until the ramen skillet thickens.

45. Crunchy Japanese ramen

Servings: 2

Ingredients

- 1 package ramen noodles
- 2 C. thinly sliced cabbage
- 1 C. thinly sliced onion
- 2 tablespoons cooking oil, divided
- 1 teaspoon ginger powder
- 1 teaspoon sesame oil
- soy sauce

Directions

a) Cook the ramen noodles according to the **Directions** on the package. Drain it

b) Place a large pan over medium heat. Heat 1 tablespoon of oil in it. Cook in it the onion with cabbage for 4 to 6 minutes.

c) Add the noodles with the remaining oil. Cook them for 2 minutes. Stir in

d) the rest of the **Ingredients**. Cook them for 2 minutes. Serve your noodles

e) Enjoy.

46. Ramen toscano

Servings: 4

Ingredients

- 1/4 C. olive oil
- 3 (3 oz.) packages ramen noodles, packet removed
- 1/2 red bell pepper, sliced
- 1/4 red onion, sliced
- 1 small carrot, thinly sliced
- 3 C. broccoli florets
- 2 teaspoons garlic, minced
- 1 teaspoon basil
- 4 eggs, beaten
- Spice Mix
- 1/2 C. parmesan cheese, grated
- 1/2 C. half-and-half cream
- 1 tablespoon oregano
- 1/2 teaspoons kosher salt

- 3/4 teaspoons paprika

- 1/4 teaspoons dry mustard

- 3/4 teaspoons ground fennel

- 3/4 teaspoons granulated garlic

- 3/4 teaspoons granulated onion

- 1/4 teaspoons cayenne pepper

- 1 pinch sugar

Directions

a) Before you do anything, preheat the oven to 400 F.

b) Get a large mixing bowl: Stir in it the seasoning mix with 1/4 C. of olive oil. Toss the red bell pepper, red onion, broccoli florets into the mix.

c) Stir 1 teaspoon of minced garlic and basil.

d) Pour the veggies mix into a greased baking sheet. Cook it in the oven for 22 minutes.

e) Heat 4 quarts of water in a large pot over medium heat. Cook in it the ramen

noodles for 3 to 4 minutes. Remove the
noodles from the water.

f) Get a large mixing bowl: Combine in it
the beaten egg, minced garlic, grated
Parmesan cheese. Add the noodles and
toss them to coat with a pinch of salt
and pepper.

g) Grease a casserole dish with some
butter. Pour the noodles mix in it and
spread it in the pan to make the crust.
Spread the baked veggies over the
ramen crust.

h) Get a small mixing bowl: Combine in it 3
eggs, the remaining 1/4 C. Parmesan
cheese, and 1/2 C. of half and half cream.
Mix them well. Drizzle the mix all over
the veggies. Cover the pie with a piece
of foil. Cook it in the oven for 22
minutes.

i) Once the time is up, discard the foil.
Sprinkle the remaining cheese on top and
cook the pie for an extra 12 minutes.
Serve it warm.

j) Enjoy.

47. Ramen Seoul

Servings: 2

Ingredients

- 1 medium potato
- 1 package ramen noodles
- 1 green onion, sliced (optional)
- 1 large egg, beaten

Directions

a) Discard the potato skin and slice them into small dices.

b) Prepare the noodles according to the **Directions** on the package while adding the potato to it and adding 1/4 of the water needed to the pot.

c) Stir the seasoning packet and cook them for potato until it becomes soft.

d) Combine the green onion into the pot and cook them until the ramen is done. Add the eggs to the soup while stirring all the time until they are cooked.

e) Serve your soup hot.

f) Enjoy.

48. Chili ramen casserole

Servings: 4

Ingredients

- 3 packages ramen noodles
- 2 (15 oz.) cans chili with beans
- 1 (15 oz.) cans diced tomatoes
- 4-8 oz. shredded cheese

Directions

a) Pour 6 C. of water in a 3 quarts baking pan. Put on the lid and place it in the microwave for 3 to 4 minutes to heat up.

b) Use a rolling pan to crush the ramen slightly. Stir the noodles into the hot water of in the casserole.

c) Put on the lid and let it cook in the microwave for 2 minutes. Stir the noodles and cook it for an extra 2 minutes.

d) Discard the excess water from the casserole leaving the noodles in it.

e) Add the tomatoes with chili and stir them well.

f) Cook them in the microwave on high for an extra 5 minutes. Top the ramen casserole with the shredded cheese.

g) Put on the lid and let it sit for several minutes until the cheese melts.

h) Serve your casserole warm.

i) Enjoy.

49. Sweet ramen skillet

Servings: 6

Ingredients

- 1 C. bell pepper, chopped
- 1/2 teaspoons ginger
- 4 whole green onions, thinly sliced
- 1 (20 oz.) cans pineapple, undrained
- 1 lb boneless chicken breast
- oil
- 2 (3 oz.) packages chicken-flavored ramen noodles 1/2 C. sweet and sour sauce

Directions

a) Pour the pineapple juice in a measuring C. Stir in it enough water to make 2 C. of liquid in total.

b) Slice the chicken breast into 1 inch dices. Sprinkle over them ginger, a pinch of salt and pepper.

c) Place a large pan over medium heat. Heat a splash of oil in it. Stir in the ramen's seasoning packets and cook them for 30 seconds.

d) Stir the pineapple liquid mix into the pan with noodles after cutting into pieces.

e) Cook the mix until it starts boiling. Lower the heat and cook them for 4 minutes.

f) Once the time is up, stir sweet and sour sauce, pepper, onion, and pineapple into the pan. Let them cook for 4 to 6 minutes or until the veggies are done.

g) Serve your sweet ramen skillet warm.

h) Enjoy.

50. French ramen pan

Servings: 1

Ingredients

- 2 (3 oz.) packages ramen noodles, any flavor
- 2 tablespoons sour cream
- 1 (10 1/2 oz.) cans cream of mushroom soup
- 1/2 C. water
- 1/2 C. milk
- 1/4 C. onion, chopped
- 1/4 C. French's French fried onions
- 1/2 lb ground beef

Directions

a) Before you do anything, preheat the oven to 375 F.

b) Get a mixing bowl: Stir in it the crusted noodles, 1 packet of seasoning, sour cream, soup (undiluted) water, milk, and onion. Place a large pan over medium heat.

c) Cook in it the beef for 8 minutes. Drain it and add it to the noodles mix. Stir them to coat.

d) Pour the mix into a greased pan. Cook it in the oven for 22 minutes. Top the noodles pan with the fried onion and cook it for an extra 12 minutes in the oven.

e) Top it with the cheese then serve it warm.

f) Enjoy.

51. Mung bang noodles skillet

Servings: 1

Ingredients

- 1 lb lean ground beef, cooked
- 6 slices turkey bacon, chopped
- 2 (3 oz.) packages ramen noodles
- 3 garlic cloves, minced
- 1 medium red onion, diced
- 1 medium cabbage, chopped
- 3 carrots, cut into thin 1 inch strips
- 1 red bell pepper, cut into bite size pieces
- 2-4 tablespoons light soy sauce
- 3 C. bean sprouts
- light soy sauce, to taste
- crushed red pepper flakes

Directions

a) Place a large pan over medium heat.

b) Cook in it the bacon until it becomes crisp. Drain it and place it aside. Keep about 2 tablespoons of the bacon grease in the pan.

c) Sauté in it the garlic with onion for 4 minutes. Stir in 2 tablespoons of soy sauce and the carrots.

d) Let them cook for 3 minutes. Stir in the bell pepper with cabbage and let them cook for an extra 7 minutes.

e) Cook the noodles according to the manufacturer's Directions. Drain it and stir it with a splash of olive oil.

f) Stir the beef, bacon and crushed red pepper flakes into the skillet with the cooked veggies. Let them cook for 4 minutes while stirring often.

g) Once the time is up, stir the bean sprouts and Ramen noodles into the veggies mix. Let them cook for an extra 3 minutes while stirring all the time.

h) Serve your noodles skillet warm with some hot sauce.

i) Enjoy.

52. Chicken Stir Fry Ramen

Servings: 4

Ingredients

- 4 tablespoons soy sauce
- 1 tablespoon corn-starch
- 1 cup chicken stock
- 1 tablespoon vinegar
- 2 tablespoons brown sugar
- 3 garlic cloves, chopped
- 6-8 oz Ramen noodles
- 2 tablespoons cooking oil
- ½ pound chicken breast, chopped
- 1-pound broccoli, florets
- 2-3 green onions, chopped
- 2 tablespoons Sesame Seeds

Directions:

1. In a bowl, combine some soy sauce with corn-starch until it becomes lumps free.

2. Add the chicken stock, vinegar, garlic, and brown sugar, mix well.

3. Add the noodles in a large container and pour hot water over them and set aside until softened.

4. Meanwhile, sprinkle some salt and pepper on chicken.

5. Heat a wok over medium heat. Add 1 tablespoon of cooking oil and then fry the chicken until it is cooked through. When done set aside.

6. Return the wok again on heat; add some cooking oil and broccoli. Cook until it becomes tender.

7. Add the sauce mixture and toss to combine. Cook for 1-2 minutes.

8. Now, drain the noodles and put them in the wok.

9. Add the cooked chicken mixture well.

10. Transfer to a serving dish and top with green onions and sesame seeds.

11. Serve and enjoy.

53. Chicken Popcorn

Servings: 2

Ingredients

- ½ pound chicken, boneless, cut into bite able pieces

- 1 egg

- 1 ½ tablespoons miso

- 3 tablespoons corn flour

- 1-2 cups crushed ramen

- Oil for frying

Teriyaki sauce:

- 1 cup Soy Sauce

- 1 cup mirin

- 2 tablespoons vinegar

- 4 tablespoons sugar

- 2 tablespoons cornflour

- 3 tablespoons water

- Daikon, shredded

- Shredded nori

- Green onions, sliced

Directions:

1. In a bowl, add the chicken, egg and miso mix well.

2. Add some cornflour and toss to combine.

3. Add the ramen. Mix thoroughly and place aside for 5-10 minutes.

4. Heat some oil in a deep pan and add the chicken pieces.

5. Fry until they are nicely golden and crisp from all sides over medium heat.

6. When done place them on a paper towel.

7. For making the sauce, you have to take a bowl and add all **Ingredients** (except for cornflour and water) and let it simmer over medium heat.

8. Dissolve the cornflour in water and add it to the sauce by stirring continuously until it thickens.

9. Remove from the heat and serve with the chicken.

10. Top with some nori and sliced green onions.

54. Chicken and Broccoli Casserole

Servings: 8

Ingredients

- 2-3 packages ramen noodles

- 1 container cream cheese

- 5 cups milk

- 3 cups rotisserie chicken, shredded, boneless

- ½ pound broccoli, florets

- 3 cups cheddar, cheese, shredded

Directions:

1. Preheat your oven to 400 degrees F.

2. Spread half the ramen noodles in a square shaped baking container.

3. In a bowl, combine the cream cheese, milk and remaining ramen.

4. Drizzle this mixture on the top of ramen.

5. Spread the chicken and broccoli over the noodles.

6. Sprinkle some cheddar cheese on top.

7. Bake for 30-35 minutes or until the noodles are cooked thoroughly.

55. Noodle Crusted Chicken Ramen Wings

Servings: 2

Ingredients

- 1 teaspoon salt
- ½ cup corn-starch
- ¼ teaspoon baking powder
- For the wet batter:
- ½ cup corn-starch
- 1 teaspoon baking powder
- 1 cup all-purpose flour
- 3 teaspoons salt
- ½ cup water
- 1/4 cup soya sauce
- 1 pack ramen spices
- 2 packages Ramen, crumbled
- oil for frying

For the dipping sauce:

- 2 teaspoons sriracha

- 3 tablespoons vinegar

- 2 tablespoons scallions, chopped

Directions:

1. Combine the dry **Ingredients** in a bowl, and place aside.

2. Now, combine the wet **Ingredients** in another bowl.

3. Heat some oil in a deep pan and spread a paper towel in a dish.

4. Now, roll the chicken wings one by one in dry batter. Shake off the excess mixture and dip them into the wet batter.

5. Fry the wings for about 4-5 minutes, or until nicely cooked from both sides.

6. Place the wings on the paper towel.

7. Now, dip the cooked wings again into the batter and roll them in the crumbled ramen.

8. Fry again for 2-3 minutes or until crisp.

9. Now, combine the sriracha, vinegar, and scallions in a bowl.

10. Serve the wings with the sauce.

56. Pork Belly Noodles

Servings: 4

Ingredients

- 2 packages ramen noodles
- Salt, to taste
- ½ pound pork belly, cut in slices
- 3 teaspoons Chinese Five spice
- Black pepper, to taste
- 2 tablespoons cooking oil
- 2 teaspoons sesame seed oil
- 3 carrots, peeled, julienned
- 2 cups snow peas
- 3 garlic cloves, minced
- 1-inch ginger slices, chopped
- 4 tablespoons soy sauce
- 2 tablespoons honey
- 1 lemon, juiced
- 1 teaspoon cornflour

- 4-5 springs mint, chopped

- 1 cup scallion, sliced

Directions:

1. Pour 4 cups of water into a saucepan and with 1 teaspoon of salt and bring to a boil. Add the noodles and cook for 5 minutes, drain and set aside.

2. Sprinkle the Five spice, 3 teaspoons of salt and black pepper over the pork, mix until coated.

3. Heat a pan and add some oil then add the pork and cook for 4-5 minutes or until it is nicely golden. Remove from the heat and put to a bowl, place aside.

4. In the same pan, heat sesame oil and cook the carrots with snow peas. Cook for 1 minute.

5. Now, add the garlic and ginger. Sauté for 1-2 minutes then add some soy sauce, honey and juice of lemon. Let it cook until some bubbles appear. In a bowl, mix

some water with cornflour add to the pan and stir well.

6. Transfer pork again to the pan and reduce the heat.

7. Add the noodles and toss to combine. Turn off the heat.

8. Add some mint and onion.

57. Hot Pork Chop Ramen

Servings: 4

Ingredients

- 1-pound Pork chops

- 4 tablespoons Chinese BBQ sauce

- 3 teaspoons peanut oil

- 2 cups green onion, sliced

- 2-3 garlic cloves, chopped

- 1 teaspoon ginger, minced

- 5 cups chicken stock

- 3 tablespoons soy sauce

- 3 tablespoons fish sauce

- 2 packages ramen noodles, cooked

- 5 pieces bok choy, quartered

- 1 red Chile, sliced

- 8 eggs

- Cooking oil

Directions:

1. Brush the pork chops with Chines BBQ sauce and place aside for 15-20 minutes.

2. Heat some peanut oil in a saucepan over medium heat, and cook the onion, garlic, and ginger, cook for 2-3 minutes.

3. Add the stock, garlic, soy sauce, 2 cups of water, fish sauces, ginger, red chilli. Let it simmer and add the bok choy. Cook for 2-3 minutes.

4. Remove from the heat. Set side.

5. Preheat your grill over high heat.

6. Spray the pork chops with some cooking oil place them on the hot grill cook until browned.

7. Flip side and from another side for 3-4 minutes and then transfer them to a plate.

8. Divide the ramen among 4 bowls.

9. Place the bok choy over noodles and drizzle with some hot soup.

10. Place the pork chops and garnish with shredded onion.

11. Top with eggs and coriander leaves.

58. Miso Pork and Ramen

Servings: 6

Ingredients

- 2 pounds pig trotters, cut into 1-inch round shapes

- 2 pounds chicken, boneless, cut into strips

- 2 tablespoons cooking oil

- 1 onion, chopped

- 8-10 garlic cloves, minced

- 1-inch ginger slice, chopped

- 2 leeks, chopped

- ½ pound scallions, white and green part separated, chopped

- 1 cup mushrooms, sliced

- 2 pounds pork shoulder, chopped

- 1 cup miso paste

- ¼ cup shoyu

- ½ tablespoon mirin

- Salt, to taste

Directions:

1. Transfer the pork and chicken in a stockpot and add plenty of water until covered. Put it on a burner over high heat and bring to a boil. Remove from the heat when done.

2. Heat some cooking oil in a cast iron over high heat and cook onions, garlic, and ginger for about 15 minutes or until browned. Set aside.

3. Transfer cooked bones to a pot with vegetables, pork shoulder, leeks, whites of scallions, mushrooms. Top up with cold water. Let it boil over high heat for 20 minutes. Reduce the heat and simmer and cover with a lid for 3 hours.

4. Now, remove shoulder with a spatula. And place it in a container and

refrigerate. Place the lid back on the pot and cook again for 6 to 8 hours.

5. Strain the broth and remove solids. Whisk the miso, 3 tablespoons of shoyu, and some salt.

6. Shred the pork and toss it with shoyu and mirin. Season with salt.

7. Ladle some broth on the noodles and top with burnt garlic-sesame-chili.

8. Place the pork in bowls.

9. Top with eggs and other desired product.

10. Enjoy.

59. Chili Flavoured Pork and Ramen

Servings: 4

Ingredients

- 1-pound pork fillet, sliced
- 3 tablespoons chilli sauce,
- 4 garlic cloves, minced
- 1 tablespoon ginger, grated
- 3 teaspoons sesame oil
- 2 packages ramen noodles, cooked
- 2 tablespoons oil
- 5 cups chicken stock
- 2 teaspoons soy sauce
- 2 cups cabbage, chopped
- 2 green onions, sliced

Directions:

1. Take a bowl and add the combine pork, garlic, ginger, chilli sauce, and sesame oil in. Set aside for 30 minutes.

2. In a wok, heat oil and cook pork for 2-3 minutes, until browned. Remove from the heat and set aside.

3. Add some broth to the pot and boil it for 1-2 minutes. Season with soy sauce.

4. Take 4 cups and add the cabbage and noodles in.

5. Add the hot soup, pork slices and onion.

6. Drizzle chilli sauce on top.

7. Enjoy.

60. Roasted Pork Ramen

Servings: 4

Ingredients

- 2 packages egg noodles, cooked
- 3 tablespoons sesame oil
- 4 tablespoons soy sauce
- 2 tablespoons oyster sauce
- 2 tablespoons rice wine
- 2 teaspoons honey
- 1 tablespoon vegetable oil
- 1 teaspoon minced garlic
- 1 teaspoon ginger, minced
- 2 scallions, cut into small pieces
- 5 shiitake mushrooms, sliced
- 1-pound pork, cut in bite-sized pieces

Directions:

1. To a large pot, add sesame oil and cooked noodles toss to combine and set aside.

2. In a bowl, combine some honey, soy sauce, oyster sauce, and rice wine. Place aside.

3. Heat a wok over medium heat and add some peanut oil with garlic, scallions, and ginger cook for 30 seconds.

4. Add the mushrooms and cook for 1-2 minutes.

5. Add the noodles with the pork. Add the sauce mixture and mix well to combine.

6. Transfer to a serving dish and serve.

61. Ginger Flavoured Sesame Ramen

Servings: 8

Ingredients

- 3 packages Ramen, with spices

- 2-pounds beef, cut into small pieces

- 8 cups chicken broth or vegetable broth

- 2 onions, sliced

- 10-12 garlic cloves

- $\frac{1}{4}$ teaspoon chili turmeric powder

- 1 teaspoon chili powder

- 2 green chilies

- 1 teaspoon salt

- 2 cups broccoli, florets

- 4 tablespoons butter

- $\frac{1}{4}$ cup sesame seeds

- 1 tablespoon ginger paste

Directions:

1. Add the beef, ginger, sesame seeds, chicken broth, salt, chili powder, green chilies, turmeric powder, noodle spices, onion, and garlic to a slower cooker, mix well.

2. Let it cook for 5 hours over low heat.

3. Now, add the broccoli and noodles, mix well. Cook again for 1 hour.

4. Enjoy.

62. Beef Steak Veggie Ramen

Servings: 4

Ingredients

- 1-pound beef steak, thinly sliced
- 3 tablespoons cooking oil
- 1 medium red onion, sliced
- 2 teaspoons ginger, grated
- 2 carrots, peeled, cut into sticks
- 6-7 baby corn, halved
- ½ pound sugar snaps
- 2 cups mushrooms, sliced
- 2 cups broccoli, cut into length wise pieces
- 2 packages soba noodles,
- ½ cup oyster sauce
- 3 tablespoons soy sauce
- 1 cup beef stock or water
- Coriander leaves, for serving

- Sliced chilli, for serving

Directions:

1. Heat 1 tablespoon of cooking oil in a wok and fry the beef until browned (in batches), set aside.

2. Add some cooking oil to the same wok and add the onion with ginger, stir-fry for 1-2 minutes.

3. Add the carrot and cook for 1 minute.

4. Add the corn, mushrooms, broccoli, and sugar snaps, mushrooms in and fry for 1 minute.

5. Add the noodles and toss to combine, cook for 1-2 minutes.

6. Return the beef again to the wok with all sauces and stock, mix to combine.

7. Top with coriander and green chilies.

8. Enjoy.

63. Broccoli and Beef Ramen

Servings: 4

Ingredients

- 1-pound streak, sliced

- 2 tablespoons corn starch

- 2-tablespoons vegetable oil

- 2 tablespoons sesame oil

- 4 garlic cloves, minced

- 1 teaspoon ginger, minced

- 1/2 cup soy sauce

- 1/4 cup brown sugar

- 1 cup chicken broth

- Pinch of pepper flakes

- 4 cups broccoli, cut into florets

- 2 carrots, peeled and cut into small pieces

- 3 packages ramen, cooked

- 4 green onions, thinly sliced

- ½ cup sesame seeds

Directions:

1. Sprinkle some corn flour over the beef and toss to coat well.

2. Heat some oil in a pan and stir fry the beef for 4 minutes per side. Set aside.

3. To the same pan, add some sesame oil with garlic and ginger fry for 1 minute.

4. Add some soy sauce, pepper flakes, sugar and broth; let it boil for 3 - 5 minutes.

5. Add the broccoli with carrots cook covered for 5 minutes.

6. Transfer beef again to the pan and toss to combine.

7. Add the noodles and onions, mix thoroughly.

8. Sprinkle sesame seeds on top.

64. Beef Meatballs Ramen

Servings: 4

Ingredients

- 3 cups beef mince
- 2 tablespoons soya sauce
- 1 tablespoon ginger paste
- 1 teaspoon garlic paste
- Salt and pepper, to taste
- ¼ cup green onions, copped
- 1 cup sesame seeds
- 1 bread slice
- 2 tablespoons butter
- 3 packages noodles with spices
- 3 tablespoons cooking oil
- 1 tablespoon vegetable oil
- 3-4 garlic cloves, minced
- 2 tablespoons honey

Directions:

1. Add the beef, bread slice, butter, ginger, garlic, salt, and pepper to a blender, blend well.

2. Transfer to a bowl and add some sesame seeds. Mix well.

3. Make round balls with mixture.

4. Heat cooking oil in a non-stick pan and fry the meatballs until nicely cooked (in batches). Set aside.

5. Add 2-3 cups of water to a pot and let it boil.

6. Add some oil, salt, and noodles, let it cook for 2-3 minutes, drain and set aside.

7. Heat reaming oil in a wok and fry garlic for 30 seconds.

8. Add the noodles, with spices and honey in, and toss to combine.

9. Add the meatballs and top with spring onion.

10. Enjoy.

65. Stir Fried Ground Beef Ramen

Servings: 3

Ingredients

- 2 cups beef mince
- ½ teaspoon ginger paste
- 2 carrots, peeled, sliced
- 1 medium onion, thinly sliced
- 3-4 garlic, chopped
- Salt and pepper, to taste
- 3 tablespoons butter
- 3 packages noodles, cooked
- 3 noodle spices packages
- 3 tablespoons cooking oil
- 2 tablespoons vinegar

Directions:

1. Heat some butter a wok and fry the ginger paste, garlic with onion until softened.

2. Add the beef mince and cook till no longer pink.

3. Season with the noodle spices, salt, pepper, vinegar. Toss to combine.

4. Add the carrots and cook for 5-6 minutes.

5. After the carrots are cooked, add the noodles and mix thoroughly.

6. Transfer to a serving dish and serve hot.

7. Enjoy.

66. Garlic Flavoured Ramen and Fish Bowl

Servings: 2

Ingredients

- 1-pound fish, cut into bite pieces
- 2 tablespoons soya sauce
- 2 carrots, peeled, sliced
- 2 cups water
- Salt and pepper, to taste
- 2 tablespoons fish sauce
- 1 tablespoon chili sauce
- $\frac{1}{4}$ cup spring onions, chopped
- Ramen noodles

Directions:

1. Add some water, garlic, carrots, all sauces, salt, and pepper to a saucepan, let it boil well.

2. Add the fish and noodles, cook for 3-4 minutes.

3. When done add some spring onion and pour into serving bowls.

4. Serve and enjoy.

67. Tuna with Ramen

Servings: 1

Ingredients

- 1 can tuna fish
- 1 package noodles
- 1 noodle spice pack
- 2 tablespoons butter
- $\frac{1}{4}$ teaspoon salt

Directions:

1. Add 1 cup of water and salt to a saucepan, bring to a boil.

2. Add the noodles and cook for 2-3 minutes.

3. When done drain all the water.

4. Add some butter to the noodles and mix well to combines.

5. Add also some spices and toss well.

6. Transfer to a serving platter and top with tuna.

68. Slow Cooked Seafood and Ramen

Servings: 4

Ingredients

- 5 cups vegetable broth
- $\frac{1}{4}$ cup water
- 3 packages ramen noodles
- 2 carrots, peeled, chopped
- 2 cups mushrooms, sliced
- 3 green onions, chopped
- 1 bunch kale
- 4 cups shrimp
- 2-3 snow crab clusters
- 3 tablespoons noodles spices
- 1 teaspoon salt
- $\frac{1}{4}$ teaspoon black pepper
- 1 teaspoon vegetable oil

Directions:

1. Add the shrimps, carrots, mushrooms, noodles, kale, oil, crabs, onions, broth, salt, pepper, spices, and oil to a slow cooker.

2. Cover with a lid and cook at High pressure for 2 hours.

3. When done, ladle to a soup bowl and serve hot.

4. Enjoy.

69. Stir Fried Vegetables and Ramen

Servings: 2

Ingredients

- 4-5 stalks bok choy, cut into 2-inch pieces

- 3 carrots, sliced

- 2 green bell pepper, cut into thin slices

- 1 pack ramen noodle, cooked

- 1 cup fresh bean sprouts

- 1 can baby corn nuggets, rinsed

- 1 cup teriyaki baste and glaze

- 1 tablespoon vegetable oil

- 1 cup water

Directions:

1. Add some oil to a non-stick pan and cook carrots, pepper and sliced bok choy for 3 minutes.

2. Add some water with bean sprouts and corn, cook for 3-4 minutes.

3. Now, add the teriyaki and mix well. Simmer for 4 minutes.

4. Serve and enjoy.

70. Roasted Vegetables with Ramen

Servings: 2

Ingredients

- 2 packages noodles, cooked
- 2 carrots, peeled, sliced
- 1 cup broccoli, florets
- 2 packages noodle spice mix
- 3 celery stalks, trimmed
- 1 red bell pepper, sliced
- 1 cup mushrooms, chopped
- 1 onion, chopped
- Salt, to taste
- 1 teaspoon ginger, minced
- $\frac{1}{4}$ teaspoon garlic, minced
- 2 tablespoons vegetable oil
- 2 tablespoons vinegar
- 2 tablespoons soya sauce

Directions:

1. Heat some oil in a pan and fry the onion with the ginger garlic paste for 1-2 minutes.

2. Add all vegetables and stir-fry for 4-5 minutes.

3. Add some spices and soya sauce, mix well to combine.

4. Add few splashes of water and cook covered for 6-minutes over low heat.

5. Now, add the noodles and vinegar, toss to combine.

6. Enjoy.

71. Easy Vegan Ramen

Servings: 3

Ingredients

- 2 tablespoons sesame oil

- 2 eggs, boiled

- 1 teaspoon ginger, grated

- 4-5 garlic cloves, minced

- 2 tablespoons soy sauce

- 4 cups vegetable broth

- 1 cup fresh shiitake mushrooms

- 1 ½ cups baby spinach

- 2 packages ramen noodles

- 1/4 cup green onions, sliced

- 2-3 carrots, shredded

- 3 tablespoons sesame seeds

Directions:

1. Heat some oil in a saucepan and fry some ginger and garlic for 20 seconds.

2. Add some vegetable broth with all spices and soya sauce. Mix well.

3. Add all vegetables (except for green onion), stir well.

4. Cook covered for 9-10 minutes over low heat.

5. Now, add the noodles and cook again for 3 minutes.

6. Top with eggs, sesame seeds and green onions.

7. Serve.

72. Red Bell Pepper Lime Ramen

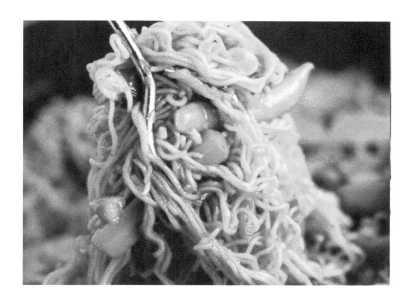

Servings: 2

Ingredients

- 4 tablespoons soy sauce

- 2 teaspoons sambal oelek

- 1 tablespoon honey

- 2 teaspoons rice vinegar

- 2 teaspoons sesame oil

- 4 teaspoons lime juice

- 1 teaspoon vegetable oil

- 2 tablespoons ginger, minced

- 1 onion, sliced

- 1 cup red bell pepper, sliced

- ¼ cup fresh chopped cilantro leaves

- 2 large bunches green onions, chopped

- 2 packages noodles, boiled with spices

- salt for seasoning

Directions:

1. Heat some oil in a pan and fry the ginger until fragrant.

2. Add the bell pepper and stir fry for 4-5 minutes or until roasted well.

3. Now, add all spices, salt, soya sauce, and sambal oelek, mix well.

4. Add also some onion and stir fry for 3-4 minutes.

5. Add the noodles, lime juice, honey, vinegar, and sesame oil, toss to combine.

6. Transfer to a serving dish and top with green onions.

73. Yakisoba

Servings: 4

Ingredients:

- Fish sauce, two tablespoons
- Egg, one
- Soy sauce, half cup
- Cooked Japanese rice, three cups
- Tomatoes, two
- Cilantro, half cup
- Salt and pepper, to taste
- Vegetable oil, two tablespoons
- Japanese chili peppers, three
- Toasted walnuts, half cup
- Chicken breast, eight ounces
- Onion, one
- Scallions, half cup
- Minced garlic, one teaspoon

Directions:

a) When the wok is very hot, add two teaspoons of the oil.
b) When the oil is hot, add the chicken and cook on high until it is browned all over and cooked through.

c) Remove chicken and set aside, add the eggs, pinch of salt and cook a minute or two until done.

d) Add the remaining oil to the wok and add the onion, scallions and garlic. Stir in all the rice. Add the soy sauce and fish sauce stir to mix all the **Ingredients**.

e) Keep stirring a few minutes, and then add egg and chicken back to the wok.

SOUPS & SALADS

74. Ramen Noodle Salad

Servings: 1

Ingredients:

- Cabbage and onion, one cup
- Sesame seeds, one tablespoon
- Soy sauce, one tablespoon
- Sugar, one tablespoon
- Vinegar, one tablespoon
- Butter, as required
- Ramen noodles, one pack
- Almonds, as required

Directions:

a) Combine the oil, vinegar, sugar, and soy sauce in a jar and shake until the sugar is dissolved.

b) Melt the butter in a large skillet over medium heat. While the butter is melting, crush the ramen noodles while still inside the package.

c) Remove the seasoning packet and throw away.

d) Add the noodles, almonds, and sesame seeds to the melted butter in the skillet.

e) Sauté while stirring frequently, until the noodle mixture is golden brown.

f) Shred the cabbage and combine the cabbage and onions in a large mixing bowl. Add the noodle mixture.

g) Pour the dressing over the salad and toss well to combine.

h) Serve immediately.

75. Baby ramen soup

Servings: 4

Ingredients

- 2 (14 1/2 oz.) cans chicken broth
- 1/2 lb baby bok choy, halved lengthwise
- 2 green onions, cut into 2-inch lengths
- fresh ginger, minced
- 1 garlic clove, minced
- 1 1/2 teaspoons soy sauce
- 1 (3 1/2 oz.) packages ramen noodles
- 1/4 lb sliced ham
- 4 hard-boiled eggs, peeled and quartered
- 1 teaspoon sesame oil

Directions

a) Place a pot over medium heat. Stir in it the broth, bok choy, green onions, ginger, garlic and soy sauce.

b) Simmer them for 12 minutes. Add the noodles to the pot. Let the soup cook for an extra 4 minutes.

c) Serve your soup warm with your favorite toppings. Enjoy.

76. Nori noodles soup

Servings: 4

Ingredients

- 1 (8 oz) package dried soba noodles
- 1 C. prepared dashi stock
- 1/4 C. soy sauce
- 2 tablespoons mirin
- 1/4 teaspoons white sugar
- 2 tablespoons sesame seeds
- 1/2 C. chopped green onions
- 1 sheet nori (dried seaweed), cut into thin strips (optional)

Directions

a) Cook the noodles according to the **Directions** on the package. Drain it and cool it down with some water.

b) Place a small saucepan over medium heat. Stir in it the dashi, soy sauce, mirin, and white sugar. Cook it until it starts boiling.

c) Turn off the heat and allow the mix to lose heat for 27 minutes. Divide the sesame seeds with noodles on serving bowls and pour the stock soup over it.

d) Garnish your soup bowls with the nori and green onions.

e) Enjoy.

77. Apple ramen salad

Servings: 10

Ingredients

- 12 oz. broccoli florets
- 1 (12 oz.) bags broccoli coleslaw mix
- 1/4 C. sunflower seeds
- 2 (3 oz.) packages ramen noodles
- 3 tablespoons butter
- 2 tablespoons olive oil
- 1/4 C. sliced almonds
- 3/4 C. vegetable oil
- 1/4 C. brown sugar
- 1/4 C. apple cider vinegar
- 1/4 C. green onion, chopped

Directions

a) Place a large skillet over medium heat. Heat the oil in it.

b) Press your ramen with your hands to crush it. Stir it in the pan with the almonds.

c) Cook them for 6 minutes then place the skillet aside.

d) Get a large mixing bowl: Toss in it the broccoli, broccoli slaw and sunflowers. Add the noodles mix and toss them again.

e) Get a small mixing bowl: Combine in it the vegetable oil, brown sugar, apple cider vinegar and the Ramen noodle seasoning packet to make the vinaigrette.

f) Drizzle the vinaigrette all over the salad and stir it to coat. Serve your salad with the green onions on top. Enjoy.

78. Ramen sesame soup

Servings: 4

Ingredients

- 1 lb top round steak, julienne
- 1 tablespoon peanut oil
- 1/2 tablespoons sesame oil
- 1 inch fresh ginger, finely grated
- 2 cloves garlic, minced
- 1/4-1/2 teaspoons crushed red pepper flakes
- 3 C. beef stock
- 2 bunches scallions, diced
- 2 tablespoons rice wine vinegar
- 2 (3 oz.) packets ramen noodles, packet removed 1/2 C. baby carrots, grated

Directions

a) Place a large skillet over medium heat. Heat in it 1/3 of each of the oils.

b) Sauté in it the ginger, garlic and red chilies. Cook them for 1 minutes. Stir in 1/3 of the beef slices. Cook them for 4 minutes. Place the mix aside.

c) Repeat the process with the remaining beef and oil until it is done. Place a large saucepan over medium heat. Stir in it the Stock, Vinegar,& Scallions. Cook them until they start boiling.

d) Lower the heat and cook it until it starts boiling. Stir in the ramen and cook it for 4 to 4 minutes or until it is done.

e) Spoon the noodles into serving bowl then top it with the sautéed beef. Serve it warm.

79. Sambal ramen salad

Servings: 2

Ingredients

- 1 (3 oz.) packages ramen noodles

- 1 C. cabbage, shredded

- 4 scallions, cut into 1 inch pieces

- 2-3 carrots

- snow peas, julienned

- 3 tablespoons mayonnaise

- 1/2 teaspoons sambal oelek, or sriracha

- 1-2 teaspoons lemon juice

- 1/4 C. peanuts, chopped

- cilantro, chopped

Directions

a) Prepare the noodles according to the instructions on the package and cook it for 2 minutes. Remove it from the water and place it aside to drain.

b) Get a small mixing bowl: Whisk in it the mayonnaise, sambal olek, and lemon juice to make the sauce

c) Get a large mixing bowl: Combine in it the cabbage, carrots, scallions, snow peas, cooked noodles, mayonnaise sauce, a pinch of salt and pepper. Mix them well.

d) Serve your salad and enjoy.

80. Cream of ramen & mushroom

Servings: 4

Ingredients

- 1 (3 oz.) packages chicken-flavored ramen noodles

- 1 (10 3/4 oz.) cans cream of mushroom soup

- 1 (3 oz.) cans chicken

Directions

a) Prepare the ramen according to the **Directions** on the package.

b) Place a large saucepan over medium heat. Stir in it the soup, chicken and seasoning. Cook them for 6 minutes.

c) Drain the noodles and divide it between serving bowls. Spoon the soup mix over it then serve it warm. Enjoy.

81. Saucy serrano ramen salad

Servings: 2

Ingredients

- 1 yellow onion, chopped

- 2 roma tomatoes, chopped

- 1 serrano chili, chopped

- 1 red pepper, roasted and peeled, medium chopped

- 1 C. mixed vegetables diced

- 2 (3 oz.) packets oriental-flavor instant ramen noodles

- 1 vegetable bouillon cube

- 1 teaspoon cumin powder

- 1 teaspoon red chili powder

- 4 tablespoons spaghetti sauce

- 2 teaspoons canola oil or 2 teaspoons any other vegetable oil

Directions

a) Place a large pan over medium heat. Heat the oil in it. Sauté in it the onion with tomato and serrano chili for 3 minutes.

b) Stir in a seasoning packet and the Maggi bouillon cube. Stir in the veggies, the cumin and 1/2 a C. of water. Cook them for 6 minutes. Stir in the spaghetti sauce and cook them for an extra 6 minutes.

c) Prepare the noodles according to the **Directions** on the package. Toss the noodles with the veggies mix. Serve it hot. Enjoy.

82. Mandarin ramen salad

Servings: 6

Ingredients

- 1 (16 oz.) packages coleslaw mix

- 2 (3 oz.) packages ramen noodles, crumbled

- 1 C. sliced almonds

- 1 (11 oz.) cans mandarin oranges, drained

- 1 C. roasted sunflower seeds, shelled

- 1 bunch green onion, chopped

- 1/2 C. sugar

- 3/4 C. vegetable oil

- 1/3 C. white vinegar

- 2 packets packet ramen seasoning

Directions

a) Get a small mixing bowl: Whisk in it the vinegar, ramen seasoning, oil and sugar to make the dressing.

b) Get a large mixing bowl: Toss in it the coleslaw mix with noodles, almonds, mandarin, sunflower seeds, and onion.

c) Drizzle the dressing over them and toss them to coat. Place the salad in the fridge for 60 minutes then serve it. Enjoy.

83. Noodles curry soup

Servings: 4

Ingredients

- 3 carrots, cut into bite-size pieces
- 1 small onion, cut into bite-size pieces
- 3 tablespoons water
- 1/4 C. vegetable oil
- 1/2 C. all-purpose flour
- 2 tablespoons all-purpose flour
- 2 tablespoons red curry powder
- 5 C. hot vegetable stock
- 1/4 C. soy sauce
- 2 teaspoons maple syrup
- 8 oz udon noodles, or more to taste

Directions

a) Get a microwave proof bowl: Stir in it the water with carrot and onion. put on the lid and cook them on high for 4 minutes 30 seconds.

b) Place a soup pot over medium heat. Heat the oil in it. Add to it 1/2 C. plus 2 tablespoons flour and mix them to make a paste.

c) Add the curry with hot stock and cook them for 4 minutes while mixing all the time. Add the cooked onion and carrot with soy sauce, and maple syrup.

d) Cook the noodles according to the Directions on the package until it becomes soft.

e) Cook the soup until it starts boiling. Stir in the noodles and serve your soup hot.

84. Creamy nuts and noodles salad

Servings: 4

Ingredients

- 1 packages chicken-flavored ramen noodles

- 1 C. diced celery

- 1 (8 oz.) cans sliced water chestnuts, drained

- 1 C. chopped red onion

- 1 C. diced green pepper

- 1 C. peas

- 1 C. mayonnaise

Directions

a) Crush the noodles into 4 pieces. Prepare them according to the instructions on the package.

b) Get a large mixing bowl: Drain the noodles and toss it with the celery, water chestnuts, onion, pepper and peas in it.

c) Get a small mixing bowl: Whisk in it the mayonnaise with 3 seasoning packets. Add them to the salad and toss them to coat. Place the salad in the fridge for 1 to 2 h then serve it.

d) Enjoy.

85. Japanese mushroom noodle soup

Ingredients

- 2oz Buna shimeji mushroom
- 1 bundle. Soba noodles or your preferred noodles. Boiled and drained according to Instructions
- 3tablespoons mizkan soup base
- 2 boiled eggs, cracked and halved
- 1 bunch baby bok choy or lettuce
- 2 cup. Water
- 2teaspoons white sesame seeds
- Scallions, chopped

Instructions

a) In a medium saucepan, boil the water and add the soup base and baby bok choy, and mushroom. Cook for 2 minutes.

b) Dish the cooked noodle into plates/bowl. Place the egg halves and drizzle the soup over it

c) Garnish with scallions and sesame seeds

d) Serve with chopsticks

86. Chicken Noodle Soup

Servings: 4

Ingredients

- 2 tablespoons olive oil

- 1 ½ cups leeks, finally chopped

- 3 garlic cloves, minced

- 1 ½ pounds chicken breast, boneless, cut into small strips

- 6-7 cups chicken stock

- Salt and pepper to taste

- 1-2 packages ramen noodles

- 1 medium lemon, cut into quarters

- 1 boiled egg, if desired

- 1 scallion, chopped, for garnishing

Directions:

1. Heat some oil in a pot over medium heat.

2. Add the leeks and garlic, stir fry until the **Ingredients** are cooked and soft by stirring.

3. Add the chicken strips and cook for about 4-5 minutes.

4. Add some chicken stock, salt and pepper, and bring to a boil. Reduce the heat and simmer the soup for 10-12 minutes.

5. Now, add the noodles and cook until firm.

6. Remove from the heat and add some lemon juice.

7. Divide the soup among 3-4 bowls.

8. Top with some scallions and egg.

9. Serve and enjoy.

87. Ramen Chicken Noodle Salad

Servings: 4

Ingredients

- ½ pound chicken, cooked and chopped
- 4-5 cups cabbage, shredded
- 3-4 carrots, peeled, shredded
- 2 packages chicken flavoured ramen noodles
- 1 cup green onion, chopped
- ¼ cup almonds, toasted, sliced
- ¼ cup sesame seeds
- ¼ cup olive oil
- ¼ cup rice vinegar
- 5 tablespoons sugar
- 3 tablespoons soy sauce
- Salt and pepper to taste

Directions:

1. In a large bowl, add the cabbage, onions, almonds, sesame seeds and ramen noodles.

2. In a mixing bowl, combine some salt, pepper, oil, vinegar, and sugar, mix well.

3. Drizzle some dressing over the salad and toss to combine.

4. Place it in your refrigerator until chilled.

5. Serve and enjoy.

88. Pork Ramen Soup

Servings: 4

Ingredients

- 3 tablespoons canola oil

- 2-3 pork chops, boneless

- salt and black pepper, to taste

- 8-10 scallions, sliced, green and white partition separated

- 1 2-inch ginger, sliced

- 8 cups chicken broth

- 3 tablespoons vinegar

- 2-3 packages ramen noodles

- 2 tablespoons soy sauce

- 2 carrots, peeled, grated

- 2-3 radishes, thinly sliced

- ¼ cup cilantro leaves, chopped

Directions:

1. Heat a saucepan over medium heat for 5 minutes. Add some oil and cook pork until cooked thoroughly, 5-6 minutes per side.

2. Season it with salt and pepper.

3. Transfer it to a plate and cover with foil. Set aside for 5 minutes.

4. In the same saucepan fry the scallion with ginger and cook for 30-50 seconds.

5. Add some broth and bring to a boil.

6. Add the noodles and cook for 2-3 minutes.

7. Stir some soy sauce and vinegar in.

8. Transfer soup to bowls and top with pork, scallion greens, chopped carrot, sliced radishes, and cilantro.

89. Easy Beef Ramen Soup

Servings: 2

Ingredients

- 1-pound flank Steak
- 1-pound Choy Sum, chopped
- 4-5 garlic cloves, minced
- 3-4 scallions, white and green separated, chopped
- 2 cups Enoki Mushrooms, sliced
- 1 1-Inch Piece Ginger
- 4 tablespoons Demi-Glace
- 4 tablespoons Miso Paste
- 3 tablespoons Soy Sauce
- 2 tablespoons Hoisin Sauce
- 2 packages Ramen Noodles, cooked
- 3 tablespoons cooking oil

Directions:

1. Add some cooking oil to a wok and fry the pork from both sides until nicely browned. Remove from the wok and set aside.

2. Add 5-6 cups of water, garlic, soya sauce, Demi-glace, ginger, mushrooms, hoisin sauce, choy chum, and scallion whites to a large pot, cook until softened.

3. Now, add the fried pork and cover with a lid, cook again for 10-12 minutes.

4. Now, add the miso and noodles, bring to a boil again.

5. Ladle to bowls and top with scallion greens.

.

90. Fish Soup Ramen

Servings: 2

Ingredients

- 2 medium fish fillets, cut into 2-inch slices

- $\frac{1}{4}$ cup spring onion, chopped

- 3 carrots, peeled, sliced

- 2 packages ramen noodles

- 1 teaspoon salt

- 4-5 garlic cloves, minced

- 2 tablespoons cooking oil

- $\frac{1}{4}$ teaspoon black pepper

- 4 cups chicken broth

- 2 tablespoons soya sauce

- 2 tablespoons fish sauce

Directions:

1. Add the chicken broth, garlic, cooking oil, salt, and pepper to a saucepan and let it boil.

2. Add the carrots, cook covered for 5-8 minutes over medium heat.

3. Add the fish, onion, and noodles, cook for 3-4 minutes or until done.

4. Add some fish sauce and soya sauce, mix to combine.

5. Serve hot.

91. Shrimps Noodle Soup

Servings: 1

Ingredients

- 5-6 shrimps
- 1 pack noodles, with spices
- ¼ teaspoon salt
- 1 tablespoon vegetable oil
- 2-3 garlic cloves, minced
- 2 cups chicken broth

Directions:

1. Heat some oil in a saucepan, and fry some minced garlic for 30 seconds.
2. Add the shrimps and stir fry for 4 minutes.
3. Add all spices, noodles, and water, bring to a boil for 3-4 minutes.
4. Put to a serving bowl.

92. Ramen Soup with Mushrooms

Servings: 2

Ingredients

- 2 cups spinach leaves
- 2 pack ramen noodles
- 3 cups vegetable broth
- 3-4 garlic cloves, minced
- $\frac{1}{4}$ teaspoon onion powder
- Salt and pepper, to taste
- 1 tablespoon vegetable oil
- $\frac{1}{4}$ cup spring onion, chopped
- 3-4 mushrooms, chopped

Directions:

1. Add the vegetable broth, salt, oil, and garlic to a saucepan and boil for 1-2 minutes.

2. Now, add the noodles, mushrooms, spring onion, spinach, and black pepper, cook for 2-3 minutes.

3. Enjoy hot.

93. Mushroom Ramen Soup

Servings: 2

Ingredients

- 2 cups mushrooms, sliced
- 2 packages ramen noodles
- 1 teaspoon black pepper
- 2 tablespoons hot sauce
- 2 tablespoons soya sauce
- 1 tablespoon Worcestershire sauce
- ¼ teaspoon salt
- 3 cups vegetable broth
- 1 onion, chopped
- 2 tablespoons chili sauce
- 2 tablespoons peanut oil

Directions:

1. Heat oil in a saucepan and stir-fry the mushrooms for 5-6 minutes over medium heat.

2. Add the broth, salt, pepper, hot sauce, Worcestershire sauce, onion, and soya sauce, mix well. Boil for few minutes.

3. Add the noodles and cook for 3 minutes.

4. When done transfer to a serving bowl and top with chili sauce.

5. Enjoy.

94. Noodles & Pork Balls with Microgreens

Servings: 4

Ingredients

Ginger Pork Balls:

- 1 pound ground, sustainably raised pork

- 1/4 teaspoon white pepper

- 1/4 teaspoon sugar

- 1/4 teaspoon onion powder

- 1 teaspoon kosher salt

- 1 teaspoon ginger, grated

- 1 tablespoon shallot, minced

- 1/2 tablespoon scallions, finely chopped

- 1 tablespoon avocado or olive oil

Noodles:

- 2 teaspoons freshly grated ginger

- 1/2 tablespoon shallot, minced

- 3 teaspoons fish sauce

- 2 teaspoons rice wine vinegar

- 4 1/2 cups vegetable stock

- 1 lemongrass stalk cut into 4 sections

- 1 teaspoon lime zest

- 6 ounces ramen noodles

- 2 1/2 tablespoons soy sauce

- 2 teaspoons chili paste

- 1 cup watercress

- 1 English cucumber, thinly sliced

- Sesame seeds, for garnish

Directions

a) In a medium-sized bowl, add all **Ingredients** for pork balls, besides oil.

b) Combine **Ingredients** with your hands, making sure shallots and scallions are distributed throughout mixture.

c) Put a little oil on your fingers to help with pork sticking to your hands. Pinch off a small amount of pork, roll into a ball and set aside on a plate.

d) Drizzle avocado oil in a large pot, over medium-high heat. Once oil is hot, add pork balls, being careful not to crowd the pan.

e) Fry in batches, until balls are brown on all sides, turning once; about 5 minutes. Set aside.

f) In same pan, add ginger and shallots. Add more oil if pan is too dry after frying. Sauté until fragrant, about 2 minutes.

g) Add fish sauce and vinegar, stirring 1 minute.

h) Add stock, lemongrass and lime zest. Stir and bring to a simmer. Add pork balls. Cover, and let gently simmer about 10 minutes.

i) Uncover and bring to a boil. Add ramen noodles and boil   5 minutes.

j) Meanwhile, in a small bowl, whisk together sambal oelek and soy sauce. Add to pot, stirring gently. Remove lemongrass from pot and turn off heat.

k) Add watercress, stirring   gently, letting it wilt.

l) Serve noodles in shallow bowls, dividing equally and adding extra broth to the bowls.

m) Top with cucumbers, sesame seeds and additional sprigs of watercress, if desired.

DESSERTS

95. Ramen With Chocolate Syrup

Ingredients

- 1 cup of brown sugar

- 1 package of Ramen Noodles

- 1 t vanilla

- 2 cups of water

- 1 cup of chocolate syrup

- Confectioners sugar (optional)

- Whipped topping (optional)

Directions-

1. Bring water to a boil in a medium sized pot. Add 1 package of Ramen Noodles. Save the seasoning for another day. Add 1 cup of brown sugar. Wait 10 minutes stirring occasionally.

2. Drain water. Put the pot back on medium heat and add 1 cup of chocolate syrup and 1 teaspoon of vanilla.

3. Stir occasionally. After waiting 5 minutes, take off heat and put in

refrigerator for 1 hour. Serve and top with confectioners sugar and/or whipped topping.

96. Ramen with strawberry sauce

Ingredients

- 1 package ramen noodles (minus seasoning packet)

- strawberry sauce (like you would get on an ice cream sundae)

- 1 bottle honey

- 1 dash cinnamon

- 1 dash sugar

- whipped cream, from a can or Cool Whip, is best.

Directions

1. Cook ramen according to package **Directions**.

2. Drain.

3. Place noodles in fridge until chilled.

4. Remove from fridge and place on a plate.

5. Add as much honey as desired, use a squeeze bottle for this.

6. Sprinkle on some cinnamon and sugar.

7. Add a drizzling of strawberry sauce.

8. Top with copious amounts of whipped cream and one more drizzling of strawberry sauce for colour.

9. Enjoy!

97. Crunchy ramen noodles Bar

Ingredient

- 6 tablespoons salted butter

- 7 c. miniature marshmallows

- 1 teaspoon vanilla extract

- ⅔ c. creamy peanut butter

- 4 (3-oz. each) ramen noodles, dry, without seasoning, and broken up

- 3 c. crispy rice cereal

- 1 c. semisweet chocolate chips

Directions

1. Spray a 9x13-inch baking pan with non-stick spray. Set aside.

2. Melt butter in a large saucepan. Add marshmallows and stir until melted and smooth. Stir in vanilla extract and remove from heat.

3. Stir peanut butter into marshmallow mixture. Fold in dry ramen noodles and

cereal until well combined. Press mixture into prepared pan. Cool 15 minutes.

4. Melt chocolate chips in the microwave until melted and smooth. Drizzle on top of bars. Cut into 24 bars.

98. Buckeye ramen haystacks

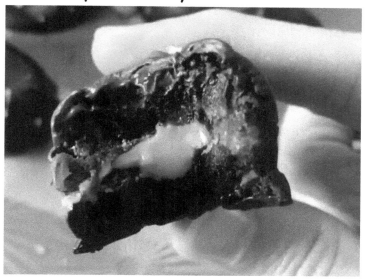

Yields 12 Clusters

Ingredients

- 1 cup peanut butter

- 8 ounces semisweet or dark chocolate chips

- 1-3 ounce package ramen, any flavor, discard the flavor packet

Directions

1. Break ramen into smaller pieces and set aside.

2. Place wax paper on a baking sheet and set aside.

3. In a medium saucepan over low heat, combine peanut butter and chocolate and stir frequently until melted and smooth.

4. Add ramen pieces and stir to combine and coat completely.

5. Remove from heat and drop by rounded tablespoon onto prepared baking sheet.

6. Place in fridge to set completely. Then enjoy!

99. Ramen Noodle Cookies

Serves 2

Ingredients

- 3 package ramen noodles any flavor

- 1 package regular size white chocolate chips

- 2 tablespoons of butter

- 1 package regular size m&m's

- 1 c raisins

Directions

1. Lay a piece of parchment or wax paper in your work area.

2. Break the Ramen noodles into small pieces and place in a bowl. Put the flavor packets aside for another use.

3. In a skillet add the butter and let it heat up till it is light brown. Add the noodles till they get all brown

4. Melt your white chocolate in the microwave or a double broiler till it is

soft and you can combine the other **Ingredients**.

5. Add the raisins, m&m's and the noodles and combine well with the white chocolate.

6. Drop the mixture by spoonfuls on to the piece of parchment or wax paper and let set until the cookie hardens and then store in a cool dry container.

100. fried-ice-cream-ramen

Ingredients

- 1 package Ramen Noodles, any flavor

- 8 scoops Vanilla Ice Cream, divided

- 1/4 c. almonds, finely chopped

- 1/2 cup honey

- 4 Tablespoons Chocolate Syrup

- Whipped cream, optional

- 2 Tablespoons Butter

- fried-ice-cream-ramen

Directions

1. Heat butter in a small skillet, adding dry, crushed ramen noodles. Sauté the ramen until crispy and lightly brown.

2. Reduce heat slightly and add honey to the sautéed ramen, stirring gently until it starts to bubble. Add finely chopped almonds. Pour over 4-6 bowls- each containing Double scoops of vanilla ice cream.

3. Drizzle each "Fried Ice cream" with 1 tablespoon of Chocolate syrup. Add a dollop of whip cream to the top and serve immediately.

CONCLUSION

What a ride! Knowing awesome Japanese meals at once was worth the ride... and if you are planning on hosting an Asian-theme party, it is a good time to start practising your Asian culinary skills and be proud of yourself. So, feel free to try your hands on them one by one and remember to tell us how it went.

Japanese Cuisine is known for its variety of dishes and its vast combination of rare spices that are usually grown only in Japan.

Happy Cooking Japanese Food!